Soviet Union

the land and its people

James Riordan

Macdonald Educational

Contents

The largest country in the world

The land

The Soviet Union sits astride two continents: Europe and Asia. It stretches from the Baltic Sea in the west a quarter of the way round the world to the Pacific Ocean in the east, within a few kilometres of Alaska and Japan. It includes most of the frozen Arctic and reaches south into hot deserts bordering on Iran.

It is by far the largest country in the world, covering a sixth of the Earth's land area. Its European part alone is equal in size to all the states of Europe combined, yet two-thirds of its territory lie outside Europe, on the rolling plains and in the forests of Asia.

The land is so vast that the day begins in the east 11 hours before it reaches the west: as people in Moscow are going to bed, those in Vladivostok are having breakfast the next day. Even in this age of speedy travel it takes over a week by train from Riga on the Baltic to Vladivostok on the Pacific. You can travel to Verkhoyansk in Siberia where the temperature falls to 70 °C below zero—so cold you can hear yourself breathe as your breath crackles in the icy air—to the scorching sands of the Kara Kum

Desert in the south, where it is so hot you could fry an egg on the burning sands.

You can travel through the cotton-valley oasis of Tashkent in Central Asia to the Himalayan 'roof of the world' in the Pamirs, thrusting five kilometres up into the sky; from the tea terraces and vineyards of the Caucasus to the clear waters of the mysterious Lake Baikal in Siberia, the world's deepest lake.

It is hard to say where Europe ends and Asia begins, since the Urals' dividing line is no real barrier; the Ural hills are no more than a gentle swelling in the vast Russian-Siberian plain.

Today, as at the dawn of history, the Soviet Union stands at the boundary, at Europe's eastern gate, sharing 12 borders equally with East and West and involved in the affairs of both.

▲ The Soviet Union is the largest country in the world. It stretches across eleven time zones, and includes very many types of climate. This vast size, and the differences of

▲ The Soviet Union is the largest country in the world. It is so vast that when people in Moscow are going to bed, those in Vladivostok are having breakfast on the next day. The immense distance makes travel and communication difficult. It takes seven days to travel by train from east to west.

◄ The tundra or 'cold desert' covers the extreme north, edging upon the Arctic Ocean; much of it is in the permafrost zone which constitutes half of Soviet territory. Winters are very long, cold and dark. Here you will find reindeer, Polar bear, Arctic fox and the snowy owl.

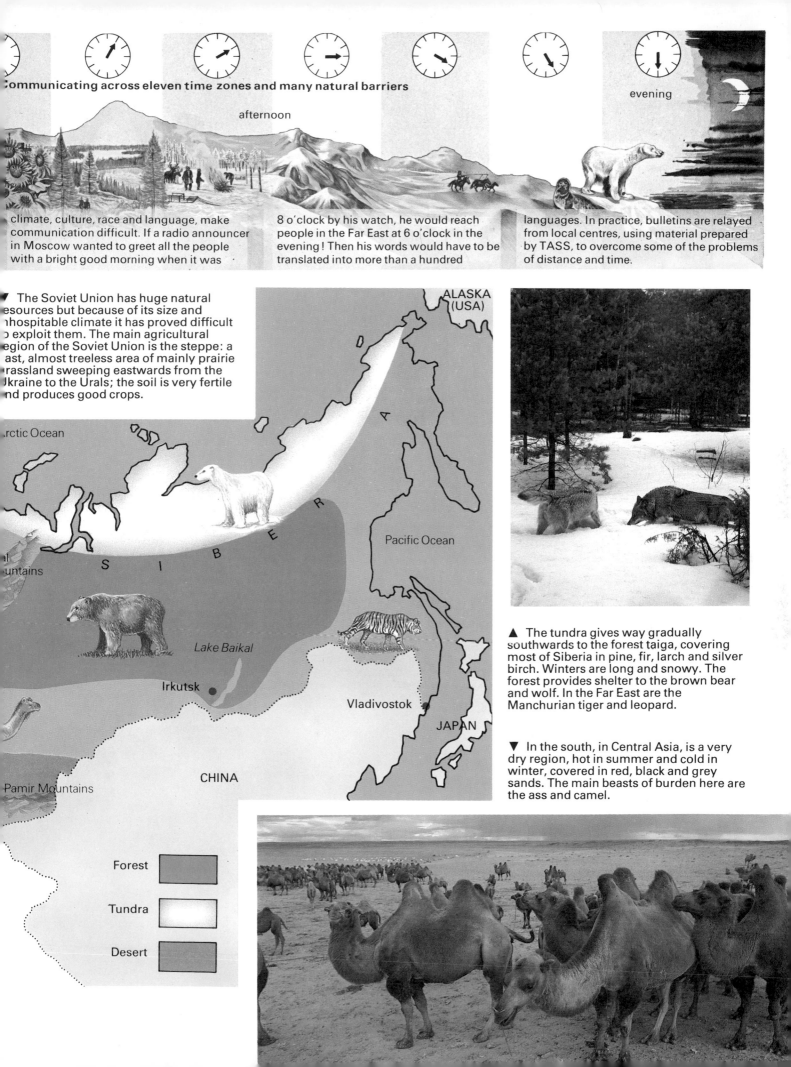

Communicating across eleven time zones and many natural barriers

afternoon

evening

climate, culture, race and language, make communication difficult. If a radio announcer in Moscow wanted to greet all the people with a bright good morning when it was

8 o'clock by his watch, he would reach people in the Far East at 6 o'clock in the evening! Then his words would have to be translated into more than a hundred

languages. In practice, bulletins are relayed from local centres, using material prepared by TASS, to overcome some of the problems of distance and time.

▼ The Soviet Union has huge natural resources but because of its size and inhospitable climate it has proved difficult to exploit them. The main agricultural region of the Soviet Union is the steppe: a vast, almost treeless area of mainly prairie grassland sweeping eastwards from the Ukraine to the Urals; the soil is very fertile and produces good crops.

ALASKA (USA)

Arctic Ocean

al untains

Pacific Ocean

S I B E R

Lake Baikal

Irkutsk

Vladivostok

JAPAN

Pamir Mountains

CHINA

Forest

Tundra

Desert

▲ The tundra gives way gradually southwards to the forest taiga, covering most of Siberia in pine, fir, larch and silver birch. Winters are long and snowy. The forest provides shelter to the brown bear and wolf. In the Far East are the Manchurian tiger and leopard.

▼ In the south, in Central Asia, is a very dry region, hot in summer and cold in winter, covered in red, black and grey sands. The main beasts of burden here are the ass and camel.

The people

Language and culture

After China and India, the Soviet Union has the world's third largest population: some 280 million. It is a vast nation of over 100 nationalities, differing in colour, language, dress and culture. Before the Russian Revolution of 1917, much of the present Soviet Union was known as Russia or the Russian Empire. After 1917 it became Soviet Russia and then, from 30 December 1922, the Union of Soviet Socialist Republics (the USSR, or Soviet Union).

The people are *Soviet*, not Russian. Though Russians make up the largest group, they comprise less than half the total population and form only one of the 15 republics. Russian is nonetheless the language of communication which everyone learns in school, like English in the USA or Britain; but most Soviet people speak their own native language as well as Russian, and school lessons are taught in their native tongue.

The three main Slav groups, the Russians, Ukrainians and Belorussians, make up two-thirds of the Soviet population. Although differing in dialect and culture, they adopted the Greek Orthodox branch of Christianity in 988 AD and modified it into Russian Orthodoxy under a Russian religious leader or 'Patriarch'. A century before, two Greek monks, Cyril and Methodius, had come from Byzantium to give the Russian language a written alphabet based on Greek.

The second largest group of related peoples after the Slavs is the Turkic or Tartar family, including Uzbeks, Tartars, Kazakhs, Azerbaidzhanis, Kirgiz and Turkmenians. They mainly live in the south, all speak a variation of the same language and share Muslim traditions.

The three Baltic peoples: Latvians, Lithuanians and Estonians, live in the north-west of the country. Part of the Russian Empire since the 18th century, Lithuania, Latvia and Estonia became independent in 1918, then part of the USSR in 1939.

Down in the Caucasus are two of the oldest one-time Christian kingdoms in the world: Georgia and Armenia. Many other groups inhabit the Soviet Union: Gypsies and Eskimos, Germans and Jews, Moldavians and Tadzhiks; not simply tiny pockets in a Russian topcoat, but large communities proud of their own identity in one of the world's most colourful families of nations. The aim has been to convert all peoples, not into Russians, but into builders of socialism.

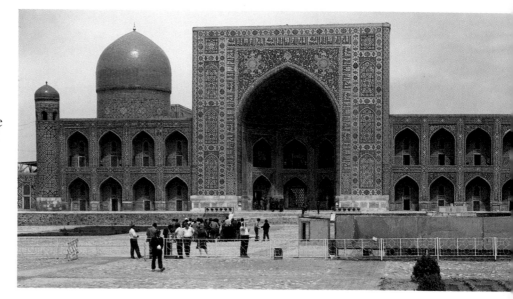

▲ The main mosque in Samarkand. The Moslem faith was adopted by Genghis Khan to bind together all the tribes of his Golden Horde; it is the Horde's descendants living in the south who today retain Islamic culture.

▼ A five-ruble note (roughly equal to five pounds or dollars) has printed on it all the languages and scripts of the 15 Union Republics.

▼ An icon of St George, formerly the patron saint of Moscow. Icons are religious paintings which are found in Orthodox Christian churches throughout the world. They are often mounted on a splendid gold screen called the 'iconostasis' which separates the nave and the sanctuary. At one time, such religious paintings with a light burning before them, were to be found in many Russian homes.

The Soviet nationalities and where they live

People in major national groups

Russians 138m
Ukrainians 43m
Uzbeks 13m
Belorussians 10m
Kazakhs 7m
Tartars 7m
Azerbaidzhanis 6m
Armenians 5m
Georgians 4m
Moldavians 3m
Lithuanians 3m
Tadzhiks 3m
Turkmenians 2m
Germans 2m
Kirgiz 2m
Jews 2m
Latvians 1.5m
Estonians 1m

Russians
Ukrainians
Moldavians
Kazakhs
Belorussians
Latvians
Armenians
Tadzhiks
Tartars
Kirgiz
Turkmenians
Uzbeks
Georgians
Estonians
Lithuanians
Azerbaidzhanis
Thinly populated areas

▼ Although many townspeople today wear standard European dress, in the countryside, especially at festivals, the many different nationalities love to dress up in their folk costumes, sing, dance and tell old tales. The people in the pictures are (top left) Uzbek, (bottom left) Russian, (centre) Chukchi from the frozen north, and (below) Armenian.

11

Russia appears on the map: Kiev Rus

Red, Black and White Russians

The first Russian state, Kiev Rus, took shape in the 6th century AD when the Slav tribes of Central Europe spread outwards from their homelands. Those Slavs remaining in the west eventually formed the states of Poland, Czechoslovakia, Bulgaria and Yugoslavia. The three tribes that trekked eastwards—known as the Red, Black and White Russians after their facial appearance (and later to be called Russians, Ukrainians and White or Belorussians) found themselves upon the vast Eurasian plain with virtually no barrier in their path east, north or south—no sea as around the USA or Britain; no mountains as in India or China, except at the distant margins—outside the original Russia which grew outwards towards them.

Whereas the West Europeans inherited much of Roman culture, the eastern Slavs found no inheritance upon their desolate plain, open to the eastern winds and nomadic invasions from groups such as the Huns, Scythians and the Goths. At the first sign of danger the eastern Slavs would spread out over the endless steppe or go deeper into the forest. While the more enterprising westerners became farmers, craftsmen and merchants, the bolder souls in the east became Cossacks and pioneers. They halted only when the land tilted upwards into mountains or dropped down to meet the sea.

In the early years the Slav settlers came into contact with the Vikings in the north and Greeks in the south, as both made their journey for trade and adventure along rivers such as the Don and Volga and via cities such as Kiev, Novgorod and Astrakhan.

Kiev Rus was destroyed in 1240 by the Golden Horde of Mongol-Tartars. Under their leader, Genghis Khan, the Horde had come from the Gobi Desert in what is now Mongolia to overrun Russia, China and much besides. The Horde occupied the land of Rus for some 300 years—until the first Russian tsar Ivan the Terrible sacked the Tartar stronghold of Kazan in 1552.

The Tartar occupation cut Russia off from the rest of Europe, so that vital developments elsewhere, like the Reformation and Renaissance, passed Russia by. Russia remained a backward, peasant state cut off from the rest of the world.

▲ The great Mongol chieftain Genghis Khan (1162–1227). His armies overran China and swept through central Asia to threaten the Byzantine Empire. It was Genghis' grandson Batu Khan who began the invasion of Russia or the 'western lands' in 1237, and eventually conquered China too.

SLAVS

Novg[o]

Kiev Rus · Moscow·

Byzantium

River Don

River Vol[ga]

Astrakha[n]

BYZANTINE INFLUENCE (GREEK)

◄ A painting by Vasnetsov called *The Bogatyrs* (1898). Bogatyr means warrior. This picture shows three folk-heroes of early Russian history, when Kiev Rus was the centre of Russian civilization. Although Kiev Rus was rich, its greatness only lasted for 300 years until it was destroyed by the Mongols.

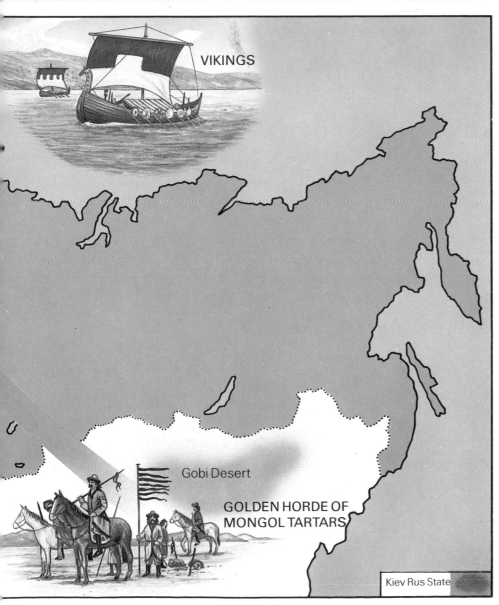

VIKINGS

Gobi Desert

GOLDEN HORDE OF MONGOL TARTARS

Kiev Rus State

▲ A 16th century print of a fortified monastery in medieval Russia. The buildings were made of wood and frequently burnt down.

◄ The lands now forming the Soviet Union have been settled by many different peoples. Slavs and Norsemen were among the early arrivals. The civilization of Byzantium spread from the south and gradually all the cultures merged.

Great Russian tsars

Ivan the Terrible (ruled 1533–84)
Ivan was the first man to crown himself tsar, in 1547. Besides defeating the Tartars, he expanded his realm westwards and established trade with England after a visit by English sailors to the new capital Moscow in 1553. Ivan's defeat of the Tartars and desire for contact with the West helped shift Russia's focus from Asia to Europe. His ruthlessness earned him the name Terrible.

Peter the Great (ruled 1682–1725)
The greatest of all the tsars and first of the last great Romanov dynasty, he opened 'a window on the West' by gaining a port on the Baltic. He did so by defeating the Swedes at Poltava in 1709 and building a beautiful new capital named after him: Saint Petersburg (now called Leningrad).

With the help of thousands of foreign craftsmen, he set about modernizing his backward country. He created a modern army and navy, made Russia a world power for the first time and introduced many reforms that helped to westernize the country. In so doing, he made the Church and nobles serve the crown.

Catherine the Great (ruled 1762–96)
Catherine was a German princess, married at 15 to Peter III, heir to the Russian throne. She had her husband murdered and took over herself, ruling for 34 years. At first she tried to apply liberal Western ideas to govern backward Russia, though ruling with a rod of iron.

Frightened by the peasant revolt led by Pugachov (1773–75) and the French Revolution of 1789, she became more conservative. While the rich, land-owning nobles lived in luxury, speaking French rather than Russian, most Russian people were serfs, little better than slaves, and badly treated by the landowners.

In foreign affairs Catherine's reign marked a turning point, as Russia expanded eastwards towards the Pacific Ocean, westwards to swallow much of Poland, and southwards to the Crimea and the northern coast of the Black Sea, displacing Turkey.

▲ A painting of Peter the Great at the battle of Poltava against the Swedes. Peter was determined to gain land then held by Sweden, to give Russia a Baltic Sea port.

▼ Although Napoleon captured Moscow in 1812 he could not make the Russians surrender and he had to retreat, leaving Tsar Alexander I a powerful ruler.

The Russian empire expands through Peter's conquests

▦ Russian territory 1689	⌇ Russian boundary 1725
▦ Russian gains 1721	
➤ Charles XII attack lines	

Peter's greatest enemy was Charles XII. At the beginning of the long war the Swedes defeated Peter at Narva. But the Swedes were finally crushed.

▲ Catherine the Great (1762–96) was as anxious as Peter to develop Russia along Western lines, and like him wanted to make Russia a European power.

▼ The Cathedral of the Assumption, in Moscow, was built in the 15th century as the private church of the Tsars but ordinary people could worship there too.

▲ Ivan IV, the Terrible (1533–84). He was the first Russian ruler to call himself Tsar. He was a successful military leader and developed trade with the West. But he was brutally cruel.

15

Fall of the Russian Empire

By the middle of the 19th century Russia was deep in crisis. Its foreign policies were a failure and at home peasant protests against serfdom were growing. Also the state could no longer bear the financial burden of supporting a noble class. Alexander II (1855–81) saw no alternative but to free the serfs, which he did in 1861. No longer would they be the property of the nobles.

Yet it was too late to save the regime. Some army officers—the Decembrists—had tried to rebel on 14 December 1825; others who favoured change (the Narodniks) went 'to the people' to gain support; yet others took to killing the country's leaders, like Alexander, who was blown up in 1881. Meanwhile, in the countryside, peasants were taking their revenge for centuries of abuse by burning down the manors. In the towns, workers in the growing number of factories were beginning to organize and go on strike for better conditions.

The situation worsened in the reign of the last tsar of the Romanov dynasty, Nicholas II, and his German-born wife Alexandra.

The 'Bloody Sunday' events of 1905 led to the setting up of workers' councils (soviets—the Russian word for 'council'), a general strike and, later in the year, an uprising that was crushed after a week of bloody fighting.

The 1905 Revolution was put down. But Russia's entry into World War I as the ally of Britain and France against Germany in 1914 made things worse. Riots by starving people took place in February 1917; these quickly spread, forcing the tsar to abdicate. (In July 1918, at the height of the Civil War, he and his family were shot.)

For eight months after the February Revolution a provisional Government ran the country, but it was then overthrown in October by the Bolsheviks led by Lenin and other Russian communists.

Lenin and the Bolsheviks

The Russian Social Democratic Labour Party came into being at the end of the 19th century, at about the same time as socialist parties elsewhere in Europe. In 1903, it split into two: the majority group, the Bolsheviks (from the Russian *bolshinstvo*, meaning majority) and the Mensheviks (*menshinstvo* meaning minority).

The Bolsheviks were led by Vladimir Lenin (1870–1924). While law student, Lenin had become a Marxist—a supporter of the ideas of socialism first set out by the German philosopher Karl Marx (1818–83), one of the authors of the *Communist Manifesto* published in 1848.

October 1917

After twelve years of foreign exile, Lenin returned home in April 1917 and at once called for a new, socialist revolution. The Bolsheviks seized power in October (November according to the new calendar adopted shortly afterwards) 1917. It was a revolution that was to shake and change the world.

◀ Lenin in his study in the Kremlin, reading a copy of *Pravda*.

▲ Tsar Nicholas II (1894–1918) with his wife Alexandra Fyodorovna. He is seen by many historians as a weak man who never understood Russia's problems. He and his family were killed in 1918.

◀ Bloody Sunday, January 22, 1905. Workers who wanted to present a petition to Nicholas II were met by troops who opened fire, killing many.

Although it looks as though the Russian cavalry is defeating the German soldiers in this World War I painting, in fact they were no match for them and there were many Russian casualties.

Soviet ideas of the world come from Karl Marx (1818–83). He saw history developing from primitive society, through slave-owning, feudal and capitalistic societies to communism. In the first phase of communist society, 'socialism', the nation owns the land, factories and mines, which are worked for the common good.

Lenin addresses a meeting of troops and workers in Petrograd. After successfully launching the Revolution, Lenin worked tirelessly to achieve a socialist state. He was a gifted speaker, who could inspire an audience. Here, he speaks under the flag of the Bolsheviks, the Red flag which is the symbol of socialism. In the early days of Lenin's rule, the Soviet Union was still subject to unrest and upheaval.

► At first, it seemed that Lenin's Government would not survive. Lenin had made an expensive peace with Germany and many people within the country were opposed to the Bolsheviks. Soon the anti-Bolshevik groups formed so-called 'White Armies' and launched a civil war. Here soldiers of the Red Army crowd on to the roof of a train as transport was so bad. By 1920 the White Armies had been defeated and peace restored.

The Soviet Union

From being an absolute monarchy at the start of 1917, Russia became a republic inspired by the ideals of socialism in November 1917. It would be hard to find such a sharp turn in history anywhere else.

The evening after the Revolution a Congress of Soviets approved decrees calling for an immediate peace treaty with Germany, giving the land to the peasants and setting up a new Soviet Government headed by Lenin. In the months to come the new government was to take over all banks, factories and transport, making what were seen as the first steps to socialism.

The hopes for peace of the millions of Soviet people were shortlived: civil war broke out—Red Guards against White. Soviet Russia was invaded by foreign troops, including British and American, and millions of people starved.

Nonetheless, Soviet Russia and the Bolsheviks, now having changed their name to the Communist Party, survived. Lenin died in 1924. During the years to follow Joseph Stalin came to dominate the country, having most of his rivals executed. At the end of the 1920s the Soviet Union embarked upon a series of Five-Year Plans designed to modernize and

industrialize it along socialist lines, with public ownership of all the factories. In the countryside, the 25 million small peasant farms were reorganized—often by force—into large collective and state farms.

This programme, carried out with no foreign aid and against the background of the growing threat of war, was accompanied by the killing, torture and imprisonment in labour camps of many millions of opponents—both real and imagined—in the late 1930s.

By the time of the Nazi attack on the Soviet Union in June 1941, the country had become a strong industrial power. It defeated the

invaders after a terrible struggle in which over 20 million Soviet men, women and children died.

By the end of the war, in 1945, the Soviet Union was one of the superpowers, its influence having extended into central Europe.

When the country developed its own atom bomb in 1949 and gained several new allies in Eastern Europe and Asia, the Soviet people felt they could no longer be so easily attacked by foreign powers and they began to live a more open and comfortable life.

Stalin died in 1953 and was succeeded first by Nikita Khrushchov and then by Leonid Brezhnev. Mikhail Gorbachov became leader in 1985.

▲ Lenin with Stalin. Lenin came to distrust Stalin and tried to prevent him succeeding as leader. Stalin kept in the background until Lenin died.

▼ The turning point of World War II for the Soviets—the battle for Stalingrad (1942–3)—when the Germans were halted and gradually driven back.

Lev Trotsky (1879–1940) was one of the ablest of the Russian revolutionaries. He joined the Bolsheviks just before the first 1917 revolution and was a key member of the first communist government, having planned the tactics of the October Revolution and then welded together the new Red Army. After Lenin's death in 1924 Trotsky was pushed out by Stalin, exiled and eventually assassinated by a Stalinist agent in Mexico.

In 1956, Soviet leader Nikita Khrushchov, a former miner and son of Russian peasants, denounced Stalin's policies. Life in the Soviet Union became freer and more pleasant. But Khruschov made political and economic mistakes and he was dismissed in 1964. He died in Moscow in 1971.

▲ Mikhail Gorbachov took over as Soviet leader on the death of Chernenko in 1985. A shrewd man, much younger than Chernenko, he at once tried to reform the economy and improve relations with the West. He met US president Reagan at a summit meeting in Geneva in November 1985.

▲ Women during the seige of Leningrad. During World War II this city was nearly encircled by German troops for 900 days. The people refused to surrender despite the most terrible conditions. These women, carrying their few possessions, had been made homeless by the bombardment. In January 1944, the Red Army drove the Germans back.

19

Place in the world today

In the space of a lifetime the Soviet Union has come a long way: through three revolutions and two terrible wars, from a land of mainly illiterate peasants to the pioneer of space travel, sending the first man and first woman into space. The Soviet people have lifted themselves out of a feudal, medieval past into the forefront of the world's great powers.

Politics

In politics, the Revolution of October 1917 inspired many people of Africa and Asia to fight for independence from their colonial rulers. It also inspired working people of other nations to try to build a socialist society in their own countries. Some, however, like Poland, Hungary, East Germany and Rumania had a Soviet-type system thrust upon them in the aftermath of the last war. Others, like Yugoslavia, China, Cuba and Vietnam, had their own popular revolutions inspired by the ideals of socialism.

Many see the Soviet system as a communist dictatorship. They point to its restriction on individual freedoms and the harsh treatment meted out to those who voice dissent. In fact this has in part been present throughout Russian history, as well as being the product of Soviet development and the need to organize a huge number of people to work towards common economic and social goals.

Economy

In economic terms, the Soviet Union has progressed from a backward agricultural land to an advanced, if unevenly developed, industrial nation. In living standards and technology, it is still behind many Western nations; in areas like oil, coal and steel production it has overtaken them; and it has succeeded in doing away with unemployment.

Its rapid rate of growth, achieved through central planning and public or socialist ownership (it has no private firms), has attracted many developing nations eager to modernize quickly.

НЕГРАМОТНЫЙ тот-же СЛЕПОЙ
ВСЮДУ ЕГО ЖДУТ НЕУДАЧИ И НЕСЧАСТЬЯ·

▲ 'An illiterate man is just like a blind man'. Having inherited a mainly backward population that could neither read nor write, Soviet leaders encouraged literacy.

▼ Both May Day (1 May) and Revolution Day (7 November) are an opportunity for parades and flag waving to celebrate the country's achievements and to express support for workers in other lands. Other festivals are more traditional.

The Soviet Union has only begun to exploit its raw materials in the last 60 years. Railways and pipelines now carry oil, coal, ores and natural gas, and great hydro-electric stations dam rivers to supply electricity for home and work.

▼ The Bolsheviks believed that their revolution was for the common person, who was regarded as the hero of Soviet society. Throughout Soviet history, its leaders have depicted the social and political unity between the factory worker and collective farmer as vital for lasting stability. The slogan reads: 'Let us build blast furnace after blast furnace'.

▲ Since their country has been invaded three times this century with enormous loss of life, and has borders with as many as 12 foreign states, Soviet leaders regard a well-equipped army as crucial to the nation's survival. All young men have to train with the army, navy or airforce.

ВЫПОЛНИМ И ПЕРЕВЫПОЛНИМ НОВЫЙ ПЯТИЛЕТНИЙ ПЛАН

ЗА 5 ЛЕТ ПОСТРОИМ, ВОССТАНОВИМ И ВВЕДЕМ В ДЕЙСТВИЕ 45 ДОМЕННЫХ ПЕЧЕЙ!

БУДЕМ СТРОИТЬ ДОМНУ ЗА ДОМНОЙ!

Arts past and present

Down the centuries, when other countries had their great writers, musicians and artists, the Russian voice was silent—apart from folk culture and Church art. It was only in the last century that Russia found its voice, and astounded the world with its richness.

In music it produced Glinka and Rimsky-Korsakov, Mussorgsky and Borodin, and perhaps the world's most popular composer of ballet and symphony—Peter Tchaikovsky.

A hundred years ago Russia gave birth to such giants of world literature as Count Leo Tolstoy, the modest doctor and playwright Anton Chekhov, the country squire Ivan Turgenev and the civil servant Fyodor Dostoyevsky. In poetry, Alexander Pushkin, grandson of an African slave, was the greatest Russian poet.

In art, Russian realist painters produced pictures that depicted the Russian countryside as well as human tragedy—Ivan Shishkin's forest scenes, Ivan Aivazovsky's seascapes, and Repin's moving human pictures such as the *Volga Boatmen*. At the end of the 19th century some artists such as Marc Chagall and Vasily Kandinsky turned to modern and abstract art.

Soviet arts

The Revolution immediately had a huge influence on the arts, encouraging experiments in all fields. But at the end of the 1920s, the arts all came under close state control, often portraying rather earthy factory and farm work, and becoming extremely patriotic. Some arts, like film and music, flourished; others, like art, architecture and much literature, found the limits of state control imposed on them restricting.

Nonetheless, the Soviet period has produced great artists, such as the composers Dmitri Shostakovich, Sergei Prokoviev and Aram Khachaturian, the film-maker Sergei Eisenstein, and writers like Mikhail Sholokhov, Vladimir Mayakovsky and the Kirgiz, Chingiz Aitmatov.

One of the greatest achievements has been the blossoming of the arts in non-Russian regions and the opening up of culture for all people to enjoy.

▲ Ilya Repin's picture of the *Volga Boatmen* (1873) earned him immediate fame with its bold illustration of the hard lot of ordinary people, like those hauling boats up the River Volga. Like other Realist painters such as Perov and Kramskoi, Repin tried to portray in his art the cruelty and suffering that existed in his native land.

▲ Marc Chagall (1887–1985) was born in Vitebsk and studied in Leningrad and Paris. He is best-known for his paintings which contain animals, objects and people from the artist's childhood, and dreams and scenes from Russian folklore.

▼ Anton Chekhov's fame in the West rests largely on his plays like *Uncle Vanya* (1897), *Three Sisters* (1900) and *The Cherry Orchard* (1903)—all three studies of the fading aristocracy at the turn of the century. This is a scene from the *Three Sisters*. Although an outstanding dramatist, Chekhov saw himself as a doctor rather than a writer.

▲ One of the greatest writers the world has ever known was Leo Tolstoy (1828–1910). A scene from his great epic *War and Peace* is shown here in a film directed by Sergei Bondarchuk.

◄ The Soviet composer Dmitri Shostakovich (1905–1975) was one of the most famous symphony composers of this century. His Eleventh Symphony, based on the October Revolution, earned him the Lenin Prize in 1958.

▼ The circus is regarded as a form of art in the USSR and is very popular; there are special circus schools to train performers. The clown Oleg Popov is loved by circus-goers the world over.

Legend and folk heroes

No country in the world has such a rich, robust, colourful folk culture as the Soviet Union, drawing upon the traditions of over a hundred nationalities.

Before radio and television, in the quietness of the long winter evenings, in a land where snow covers the ground for half the year, storytelling was a favourite entertainment.

Skilful storytellers were welcome all over Russia in people's homes, though not always by state and church, which in the 16th century had the storytellers' tongues cut out.

Even in this century, small communities are still making their own local culture in song, story, dance, art and games.

Russian folk heroes

In the depths of winter, old Grandfather Frost hands out gifts to good girls and boys, helped by the Snowmaiden Snegurochka. Within the forest, is the witch Baba Yagá, living in her revolving hut built on hen's feet, sitting on the stone stove, her crooked nose reaching to the ceiling. She rides through the air in a mortar, pushing herself along with a pestle and sweeping away her tracks with a broom.

In Russian folklore each river and lake has its spirit—old, ugly and green-bearded, who, when drunk, makes the rivers overflow and, when pleased, guides fish into fishermen's nets. But when cross, he raises storms, sinks ships, and strangles sailors. And in the depths of the waters lives the *rusalka* or water nymph, a lovely naked girl with skin the colour of moonlight, silken hair and emerald eyes. She so charms passers-by with her songs and laughter that men sometimes drown themselves for her sake.

Modern heroes

Today folklore is still popular in country areas, but city dwellers now have new legends and heroes to admire, like Lenin, the Civil War commander Chapayev, and the first man and woman cosmonauts, Yuri Gagarin and Valentina Tereshkova.

▲ Ivan Tsarevitch, the King's son, sets out on his adventures in search of a wife. Russian children still read with interest legends about the princes and princesses of pre-Revolutionary days.

▼ A green-bearded ogre guards a lake in Tartary. But a poor orphan boy, Abzelil, manages to get the better of him in three trials of skill. He is rewarded by winning a fine horse.

'Baba Yaga' is the witch of Russian folk [ta]le. Here she fails to catch the young girl, [Va]silissa, she has been fattening to eat [be]cause a river and a forest have sprung [up] to bar her way. Unlike Western witches, [B]aba Yaga is sometimes portrayed as a [st]rong and helpful character, though [al]ways ugly.

There once lived a wealthy merchant who [k]ept a nightingale in a cage. He fed the [bi]rd on choice corn and pure water. One [d]ay, however, the merchant found his pet [d]ead—or so he thought. Yet when he tossed [it] away, the 'dead' bird came to life and [fl]ew away to freedom. The moral of the [st]ory is that it is better to be free and [h]ungry than captive and well-fed.

▲ Grandfather Frost gives a little girl a present at the New Year. He looks very much like Father Christmas, although Christmas as a religious festival is no longer generally celebrated. New Year's Day is a holiday when children are given toys and some families will also buy a tree for the house and decorate it. The words on Grandfather Frost's house in the picture mean 'A Happy New Year'.

25

Inventions and discoveries

Sputniks

On 4 October 1957 the Soviet Union surprised the world by launching the first artificial satellite into space. It was called Sputnik I. The next Sputnik carried a dog, Laika, into orbit, and the spaceship Luna 3 sent back the first pictures of the far side of the moon. But the event that really caught world attention was the 108-minute flight by Yuri Gagarin, the first man in space, on 12 April 1961.

The first spacewoman was Valentina Tereshkova, who circled the earth 48 times in Vostok 6; she later married fellow cosmonaut Andrian Nikolayev. On 18 March 1965, A. A. Leonov, clad in a spacesuit, became the first man to walk in space, from the orbiting Voskhod 2. The first landing of an unmanned spaceship, Luna 9, on the moon followed on 3 February 1966.

Russian discoveries

Anyone who studies chemistry will know the table of elements invented by the Russian chemist D. I. Mendeleyev (1834–1907). His Periodic Law of Elements, published in 1870, classified known elements.

Another 19th century Russian scientist, A. S. Popov, invented radio at the same time as Marconi. Ivan Pavlov showed that reflexes can be conditioned by external stimulants. He did this in an experiment with dogs: he showed meat to a dog and at the same time pressed a buzzer, causing the dog's mouth to water in expectation of food. In time the dog's mouth would water whenever the buzzer sounded, even when no food was shown.

Ivan Sechenev (1829–1905), who was referred to by Pavlov as 'the father of Russian physiology', demonstrated that mind and body are interrelated and that by developing the body one can improve the mind. His theory of 'active rest' led to exercise breaks being introduced at workplaces to improve employees' productivity. Soviet physical education owes much to Sechenev.

▲ Ivan Pavlov (1849–1936) was a physiologist whose experiments on dogs led to the discovery of 'conditioned reflexes'. His work has had a great influence on psychology.

▲ The *Lenin* was the world's first atomic-powered ice-breaker. It was launched in Leningrad in 1957. The Soviet Union has since built even bigger ships which can break ice up to two metres thick. Since Soviet ports in the north and some rivers are frozen for many months, ice-breakers can extend the shipping and fishing season by clearing a passage for ships.

◄ Dmitri Mendeleyev, a 19th century Russian chemist, invented the periodic table: a way of arranging the chemical elements in groups on a chart. He was also able to predict the presence of new elements to fill in the gaps in the table. The first draft of Mendeleyev's table was drawn up in March 1869.

Konstantin Tsiolkovsky (1857–1935) was a self-taught scientist whose theories [o]n rockets, their fuels (such as liquid [h]ydrogen), and how they would behave in [s]pace, became the basis of modern [r]ocketry and manned space travel.

▲ On 4 October 1957 the Soviet Union launched the first artificial satellite (sputnik), which made a single orbit in space. The man mainly responsible for this 'golden day' in Soviet history was Sergei Korolyov (1906–66), who headed the rocket teams. Yuri Gagarin (1934–68) made the first space flight on 12 April 1961.

▼ Vladimir Zvorykin (1889–1982) invented television in the Soviet Union at almost the same time as John Logie Baird in England. Zvorykin's cathode ray tube television forms the basis of modern electronic systems for cameras and receivers.

Industry and technology

A wealth of mineral resources

Although only six per cent of the world's population lives in the USSR, the country produces a quarter of the world's coal and natural gas, and a fifth of the oil. It is the world's largest producer of oil and coal and second only to the USA in natural gas. Its deposits of energy sources (coal, oil and gas) are more than those of any other industrial country. It also possesses virtually every raw material and mineral in abundance, including gold, copper, zinc, lead and diamonds.

Despite this natural bounty, during the thousand years that elapsed between Russia's emergence as a political entity in the 9th century and the abolition of serfdom in 1861, the economy remained backward. That year, 1861, was the dividing line between old and modern Russia.

The industrial revolution

But it was only in the late 1920s and early 1930s that the USSR began to lay the foundations of its present-day industrial strength.

After the October Revolution of 1917, the state took over every mine and factory. From the late 1920s they were run for the nation's benefit to an overall plan—usually for five years at a time. For many years, while the economy was weak, this meant concentrating on heavy industry, building railways, steel mills, giant hydro-electric stations and dams on the fast-flowing rivers. It also meant developing backward areas; opening up the cold wastes of Siberia for coal, iron ore, natural gas and gold and dig canals to bring life to barren deserts.

During this new 'industrial revolution' life was hard and people went without many everyday necessities. Many suffered and died. But the nation was transformed from a backward rural country to a major industrial power. Unemployment was eliminated and millions of illiterate peasants were trained in new industrial skills. In 1920 80 per cent of the Soviet people still lived off the land, while in the 1980s nearly 70 per cent of the population lived in towns and cities.

◀ At the end of the 1920s the government turned the 25 million small household farms into 300,000 big co-operatives or collective farms, each based on a single village. Today there are two types of farm: collective and state. Collective farmers own their own animals, produce and tools, sell an agreed amount of their crops to the government at a fixed price, and are free to sell any surplus at market. State farms employ and pay workers as if they were in a factory.

◀ The Friendship Pipeline, which takes natural gas some 150,000 km from the frozen wastes of Siberia all the way to French homes.

▶ The vast spacedrome (*cosmodrome*) at Baikonur in the deserts of Kazakhstan is the launching site for Soviet space flights. It was from here that the world's first spaceman, Yuri Gagarin, made his famous flight.

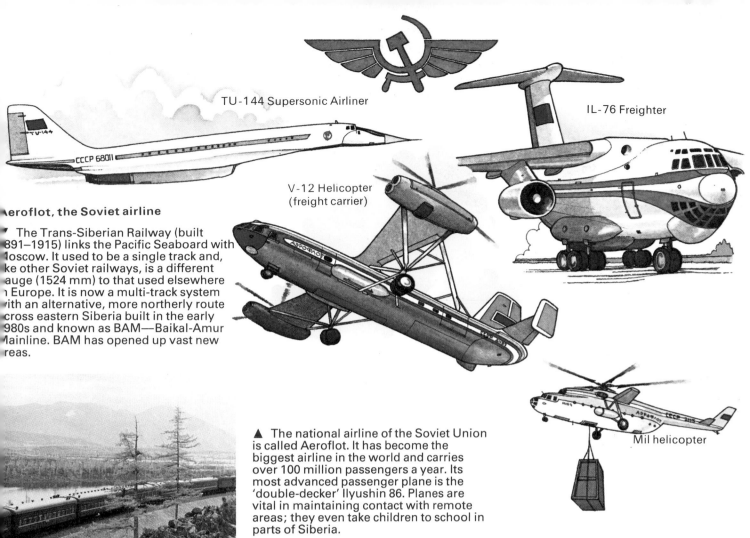

TU-144 Supersonic Airliner

CCCP 68011

V-12 Helicopter
(freight carrier)

IL-76 Freighter

Mil helicopter

Aeroflot, the Soviet airline

The Trans-Siberian Railway (built 1891–1915) links the Pacific Seaboard with Moscow. It used to be a single track and, like other Soviet railways, is a different gauge (1524 mm) to that used elsewhere in Europe. It is now a multi-track system with an alternative, more northerly route across eastern Siberia built in the early 1980s and known as BAM—Baikal-Amur Mainline. BAM has opened up vast new areas.

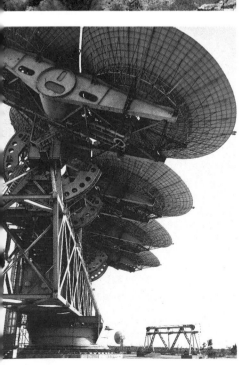

▲ The national airline of the Soviet Union is called Aeroflot. It has become the biggest airline in the world and carries over 100 million passengers a year. Its most advanced passenger plane is the 'double-decker' Ilyushin 86. Planes are vital in maintaining contact with remote areas; they even take children to school in parts of Siberia.

▼ The Kara Kum Canal (built 1954–85) takes water 1450 km across the scorching 'black sands' of Turkmenia from the Amu-Darya River to the Caspian Sea, making it the world's longest artificial river. Its 40-metre width allows steamships to travel along it.

Moscow, heart of Russia

The wooden fortress

When it was mentioned in the first written records of 1147 AD, Moscow was little more than a village. A few years later, Prince Yuri Dolgoruky had a wooden fortress built on a hill overlooking the Moscow River. After a time this was replaced by stone walls.

Moscow had by that time so far outstripped ancient rivals like Novgorod and Vladimir that it had become the chief city of a growing empire. It remained the capital until 1703, when Peter the Great moved his court to Saint Petersburg. In 1918, after the Revolution, Moscow was made capital again, this time of the Soviet Union.

Old Moscow has been rapidly disappearing as new blocks of flats and offices, broad avenues and spacious squares have been built; but in the back streets you can still find the mansions of former merchants and some old wooden houses.

The Kremlin

Moscow is planned like a spider's web within two long circles—the Boulevard Ring and the Garden (Sadovoye) Ring. At the centre is the Kremlin (meaning 'fortress' in Russian). Within its walls are the Soviet Parliament, several old cathedrals and the tsarist palace, with its treasures—now a museum.

Along one side of the Kremlin walls is Red Square, so called because the old Russian word for 'red' (*krasny*) also meant 'beautiful'; so it really means Beautiful Square. Red Square is the central point of parades, especially on traditional holidays like Revolution Day (7 November) and May Day (1 May).

The tomb or 'mausoleum' of Lenin, containing Lenin's embalmed body in a glass case for visitors to see, is also in Red Square.

No visit to Moscow is complete without a journey on the famous underground, known as the Metro—perhaps to visit Moscow University on Lenin Hills or the vast Economic Achievements Exhibition in the north-west of the city.

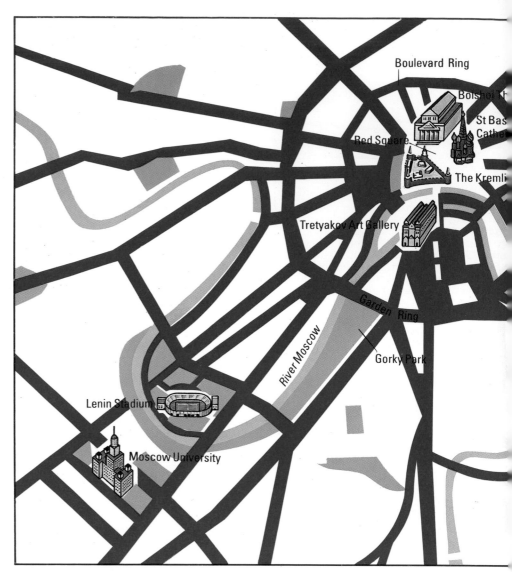

▲ New Moscow, a view along the river showing new buildings and roads. The broad embankment along the River Moskva has room for eight rows of cars!

The space between the lines in the middle is reserved for ambulances, the police and government cars. It also helps pedestrians to cross the wide road.

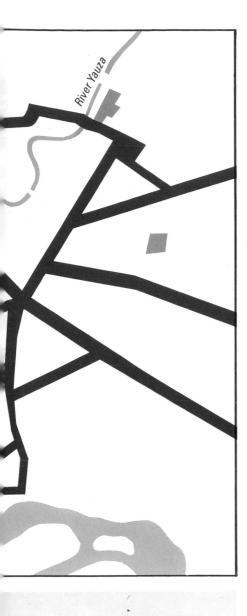

◄ A map of the centre of Moscow showing its principal buildings. Around the Kremlin are the vast GUM shop, Red Square, St Basil's Cathedral, the History Museum, the old Riding School (now a picture gallery), Lenin Library and two hotels—Rossiya and Moscow.

▼ The Moscow Metro is one of the world's most efficient, cheap (costing only about 5p to travel any distance) and extensive underground systems, with about 150 km of routes. It contains no advertising posters, but has beautifully designed and decorated underground stations.

◄ The cathedral of St Basil, Moscow, was built for Tsar Ivan the Terrible between 1555 and 1561, to commemorate his military success at Kazan. He is said to have had the architects blinded so that they could never build another church.

▲ Moscow University (founded 1755) today stands on Lenin Hills overlooking the Lenin Stadium and Moscow River. Its 'wedding cake' style of architecture was imitated in other buildings in the city, but the style is no longer fashionable.

Ballet and dance

It has been said that Russians dance as naturally as Italians sing and birds fly. Folk dancing is a popular entertainment all over the country, and many boys and girls belong to folk dance groups.

Dances like the Russian *trepak*, and Ukrainian *gopak* and *kazachok*, are today among those performed by several famous folk dance companies. The Georgian Dance Group is just one of many folk dance companies that have taken their graceful and exciting dancing abroad.

Russians have given us some of the best ballets, dancers and choreographers in the history of ballet; such popular ballets as *Swan Lake*, *Nutcracker* and *Sleeping Beauty*; such dancers as Anna Pavlova, Galina Ulanova, Vaclav Nijinsky and Rudolf Nureyev; such great choreographers as Marius Petipa and Mikhail Fokine all lived and worked in Russia. And the Moscow Bolshoi and the Leningrad Kirov are two of the world's best ballet companies.

The origins of theatrical dance in Russia are to be found in royal entertainments and folk dancing. As early as 1673 the first recorded ballet in Russia was performed for Tsar Alexei at his summer palace near Moscow. Ballets began to be staged regularly in Moscow from 1776—the year in which the Bolshoi was founded. But it was the arrival of the French-born Petipa in Russia, and his work from 1869 in designing ballet, that really changed ballet for all time. His two greatest spectacles were Tchaikovsky's *Sleeping Beauty* and *Swan Lake*.

Today Soviet ballet has almost 250 years of tradition behind it. There has been a rapid expansion of activity since 1945, with companies now established in 32 cities. The government has also done much to encourage ballet and folk dancing among the non-Russian nationalities, and many new and exciting groups and works have been created. Russian folk dancing is today performed abroad by the Beryozka, Moiseyev and Soviet Army ensembles.

▲ The ballet *Spartacus*, based on the slave rebellion against the Romans, was written by the Armenian Soviet composer Aram Khachaturian (1903–78), who also created the *Sabre Dance* and *Masquerade*.

▲ Anna Pavlova (1881–1931), the daughter of a washerwoman and a soldier, rose to become perhaps the world's greatest ballerina. She was born in St Petersburg, made her debut in 1899, and formed her own ballet company in 1909. Her most successful performances were in *Giselle*, *The Dying Swan*, *Don Quixote* and her own composition *Autumn Leaves*. She toured the world and made Russian ballet popula everywhere. Her last 20 years were spent abroad and she died at the age of 50 in Holland.

People all over the Soviet Union love dancing and a family celebration or festival is a chance to dress up in national costume and dance the traditional way. These people are from Turkmenia.

A scene from *Swan Lake* at the Bolshoi Ballet in Moscow. The standard is so high that dancers must be very experienced before taking leading roles. At the same time, the Bolshoi is criticized for being inadventurous, in failing to perform new ballets and preferring classics like *Swan Lake*.

An Armenian Dance Company, from Yerevan. They are wearing the traditional costumes of this part of the country. The dancing of the south is marked by the remarkable agility of the male dancers.

Family life

Since the late 1920s millions upon millions of country dwellers have moved into the towns and new industrial centres. Moscow grew from two million in 1917 to eight million today, and over 25 cities now have more than a million people.

In the 1920s families often had to share a flat, but now most have their own, usually with two or three rooms in tall tower blocks. Down in the south, in cities like Tashkent and Dushanbe, blocks of flats are no higher than four storeys for fear of earthquakes.

In the countryside most families still live in wooden houses, though some in Central Asia live in mud-baked *yurtas*, and some Siberians live in walrus-skin tents or *yarangas*. In some Siberian villages built upon the frozen ice, or permafrost, the wooden houses sink slowly into the ground as their heat melts the ice, so creating a topsy-turvy picture.

Life in the frozen north is quite different from elsewhere in the country; children may well travel to school by reindeer-drawn sledge or even by helicopter.

Since the state owns all land and most housing, the cost of rent and heating is low. There are no private shops, so prices of items are the same wherever you shop, apart from the street markets. Prices of staple foodstuffs tend to be low, those of items like imported fruit and chocolate are high. Because of shortages, queuing can be tedious, especially as you have to line up twice

◄ The famous State Universal Store (GUM) in Red Square, Moscow. It is really a shopping arcade on two floors, with many small shops in the bays. On the third floor, which can be seen in the far distance, are the workshops of the tailors and the dressmakers.

▲ The nomadic people of Central and Asiatic USSR live in tents made of skins. These can easily be moved from place to place.

◄ Many older houses with their little patches of garden still survive, especially on the outskirts of the towns. Sunflowers are grown here for their seeds.

once to get served and then to pay at the cash desk. The cashier usually works out your bill on an abacus or bead frame in the old way.

Most women as well as men go out to work. It is not uncommon for the own wife to have a better-paid job than her husband. Many children, therefore, go to nursery.

Weekends are the real opportunity for family leisure. In summer there are country rambles; in winter there is skating, skiing or sledding.

▲ Many old wooden houses (called *osobnyak*) still remain, especially in the villages. Three generations of one family often live together.

▲ In order to build houses quickly, prefabricated parts are used. Television aerials are frequently to be seen.

◄ A free market, near Moscow. Peasants have been allowed to keep a small piece of ground around their houses and they are allowed to sell any surplus vegetables they grow. These stalls are very popular because the produce is fresher than in the state shops, but prices are higher.

▲ In the old towns wood was often used to build big houses. Windows and doors are often decorated with ornamental patterns.

▲ In every big town you can see huge blocks of flats, built of stock designs to help solve the serious housing problem.

▼ A family in a Soviet flat. As in many modern cities, most families live in blocks of flats. A Soviet family normally has two or three rooms, plus kitchen, bathroom and hallway. Rent is about 5% of family income. Gas, phone and electricity charges are also low.

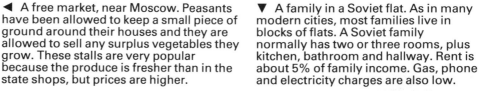

Eating the Soviet way

Soviet people are generally hospitable, and guests invited for a meal may well find a full table. In Russia, the meal may start with pickled herring, mushroom and cucumber, with some salad or caviar, accompanied by delicious black bread (which Russians prefer to white)

This may be a good excuse to chase the food down with some vodka—always drunk straight (mixing it with juice is a crime!) and in one gulp to shouts of *za zdorovye*! (good health!).

Next may come a home-made soup, perhaps *shchi* (cabbage soup) or *borshch* (beetroot soup) or *ukha* (fish soup) with sour cream added, and again with black bread and another vodka (or two). This is followed by a main course of meat or fish, often accompanied by one of the many fine wines, especially from Georgia. The meal could end with pastries and milkless tea or black coffee.

If you take a trip down to Central Asia, you may find yourself seated on the floor eating delicious lamb kebabs, pilau rice dishes and abundant fruit. It is in the Caucasus, particularly among the Georgians, however, that hospitality is at its warmest. The meal may start with cold chicken in walnut sauce (*satsivi*), melted goat's cheese (*suluguni*) with herbs (*chizhy-pizhy*) and beans (*lobio*), followed by a spicy soup like *kharcho* and the main dish of grilled spring chicken (*tabaka*) or kebab—washed down with wine or even the demon *cha-cha* vodka, and accompanied by some beautiful Georgian singing.

ZA ZDOROVYE!

▲ Delicious pastries from market stalls are often bought to eat at home. Many people also prefer to buy fresh meat and vegetables from such 'private' sources.

Make yourself a Russian meal

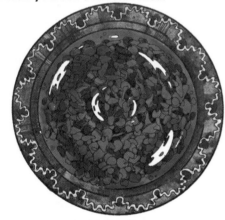

BORSHCH (BEETROOT SOUP)
14 g butter
21 g chopped onions
226 g beetroot, peeled and cut small
1 tablespoon wine vinegar
1 tomato, roughly chopped
½ teaspoon salt, little pepper
0.5 l. beef stock
113 g white cabbage (shredded)
13 g cooked brisket (cut up)
28 g frankfurter sausages (cut up)
parsley and a piece of bay leaf
sour cream to serve with soup

Melt butter in saucepan. Add onions and cook till soft. Add beetroot and other ingredients (except cabbage, meat, parsley, bay leaf and some of the beef stock). Simmer for 50 minutes. Add rest of stock with cabbage and bring to boil. Add meat and tied stalks of parsley and bay leaf. Cook for half an hour. Taste constantly and remove the herb when the flavour is strong enough. Add salt to taste. Serve with a tub of sour cream.

BEEF STROGANOV
226 g fillet of beef (without fat)
cut in small strips
113 g sliced onions
113 g mushrooms
good ½ teaspoon of mustard
½ teaspoon sugar
½ teaspoon salt, pepper to taste
1 tablespoon vegetable cooking oil
sour cream

Mix mustard, sugar and salt into a thick paste and leave for at least 15 minutes.

Heat some of the oil and cook the vegetables until soft. Drain off the oil and stand on one side. Take another pan and heat the remainder of the oil till very hot. Cook the meat for a few minutes, turning constantly. Transfer the cooked meat into the pan with vegetables and simmer them together (adding a little more oil if necessary). Stir in sour cream with mustard, salt and sugar, being careful that the cream does not curdle. Simmer for few minutes, then serve with chips.

VARENYKY
(Sweet dumplings filled with cherries)

Dough
113 g plain flour
1 egg and 1 beaten egg white
3 tablespoons milk
little salt
Mix till dough is stiff enough to form a ball. Add a little more milk if necessary. Dust with flour and chill for 30 minutes.

Cherries
226g drained sour cherries
28g sugar (or to taste)
Simmer till cherries are soft and sugar melted. Roll out dough and press out circles with a wide-rimmed glass. Coat with beaten egg-white. Put cherries in circle and fold over, pressing edges to seal. Boil pan of water simmer dumplings for about ten minutes until they float. Transfer to heated dish. On serving moisten with melted butter. Serve with cherry sauce and sweet cream.

A typical day's menu

Breakfast (Zavtrak): a boiled egg, slices of bread, and cocoa or tea without milk.

Lunch (Obyed): meat rissoles, chips, tea without milk.

Supper (Uzhin): soup; a meat dish with vegetables, tea and a sweet.

▲ A small self-service restaurant. A high degree of cleanliness is maintained and the staff wear head-scarves and overalls.

Some famous traditional dishes

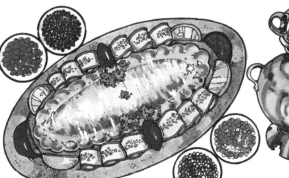

▲ An open-air barbecue. Kebabs and sausages on skewers, cooked on an open brazier, have spread north from Uzbekistan.

▲ Sturgeon in aspic, with side-dishes of different kinds of caviar. There are at least eight kinds of caviar. Caviar is the roe of the sturgeon.

▲ Pancakes like blinis are eaten with many side dishes, butter and sour cream. The samovar, seen on the left, is used to water down the strong tea, and to keep the pot warm.

▲ Chicken Kiev with a side-dish of salad. The boned chicken breast is folded over a piece of butter, coated in beaten egg and bread crumbs, then chilled and deep-fried.

▲ Gozinakh and Klava are southern sweetmeats similar to Greek and Turkish sweets, and equally delicious. Nuts and honey are important ingredients.

37

Going to school

The school day

On 1 September the school year begins after the long summer holidays. Pupils carrying flowers are met at the school gates by their teachers, and the older children welcome the new pupils who start school after their sixth birthday. It is a pleasant start to school.

School begins each day around 8.30. Very young pupils finish at midday, seniors continue to 2.30. Schools are open six days a week, including Saturdays; in some towns where there is a shortage of schools, pupils may begin school after lunch and work until early evening.

A free education

Many town children attend nursery before school. And when they go to school, they normally enrol in the one nearest home and stay for at least nine years; no one can leave before 17. Pupils remain in the same class and usually finish school with the same classmates that they met on the first day. There is no streaming or setting, no private or single-sex schools anywhere in the country.

Some special boarding schools exist for handicapped children and for those gifted in art, music, ballet, science and sport. Like all schools in the Soviet Union, these are completely free.

Children study at school in their native language—Russian, Georgian, Latvian, Tartar, Ukrainian etc.; but all children follow the same course, wear the same uniform and study from the same textbooks.

After the bell goes

Education is not over when the bell goes. All pupils are members of a youth group, and attend their clubs after school. The youngest join the Octobrists; at 10 they become Pioneers with the right to wear the red neck scarf, and at 15 they join the *Komsomol* (Young Communist League) whose motto is the same as the Scouts and Guides: 'Be Prepared'. It is the duty of the Komsomol members to help and look after the younger children.

▲ Playtime at nursery school. With almost all parents working, most town children attend nursery up to the age of six. All nurseries are state-run and the cost is low.

Soviet school system

Nursery 1-6 years

Secondary school 6-15 years

Specialist school 15-19 years (nursing, clerical, technical skills)

General school 15-17 years (sixth form)

Trade school 15-18 years (apprenticeship)

University 17+

Institute or college of further education 17+

▲ September 1, the start of the new school year, is a big occasion, with flowers, flags and the national anthem. Girls still wear the uniform of Russian schoolchildren in the last century.

▶ After school, most children go to a Pioneer 'Palace' where they follow a variety of activities, from folk dancing to woodwork, photography to sport. In summertime, many young people spend a month at a Pioneer camp in the countryside.

▼ At the age of 15 most young people go to technical college for 3–4 years; they learn a trade or profession like nursing, engineering or clerical work, and often combine study with practical experience.

Sport and leisure

Time off

In a land as vast as the Soviet Union people naturally have a variety of leisure-time activities to choose from: mountain climbing in the Caucasus or Himalayas, fishing in the many rivers and lakes—even through the ice in winter—bathing in the Baltic or Black Sea, and rambling through the fir and pine forests of Central Russia and Siberia (though watch out for wolves, bears and even tigers in the forests of the Soviet Far East!). The choice is almost endless and nowadays people have the free time and money to enjoy it. Only one in three families own their own car, but public transport is cheap and convenient.

Many families use trade union facilities at their workplace to spend an inexpensive holiday at a summer holiday camp or spa, or even in a palace, once the home of a royal prince. For millions of children in the Pioneers there are summer camps in the forests or by the sea.

▲ With the world's largest and most varied country as their playground, Soviet children have plenty of opportunities to skate, fish, ski, hike and sledge.

◄ Games of chess in a park. People take the game very seriously and follow the play of the world champions with interest. The Soviet Union produces many of the world's finest masters.

Sport for all

All young people are urged to do the national fitness programme, known as *Gotov k trudu i oborone*: 'Ready for Work and Defence'. It includes all-round ability in several sports. But if you wish to take up a sport seriously you can join a club and aim for set standards in a rankings ladder, moving up from Junior Grade 3 to Master of Sport. If you reach the Master level you can play your sport full time while studying as a PE student. The most talented athletes can attend one of the 50 sports boarding schools.

Since its summer Olympic debut in 1952, the Soviet Union has dominated the Olympic Games, summer and winter, providing many exciting champions in gymnastics, figure skating, wrestling and ice hockey. In 1980 it became the first communist country to host a summer Olympics. Despite a partial boycott led by the USA over the Soviet invasion of Afghanistan, the Moscow Olympics were extremely successful and attended by 81 nations; 74 new Olympic records were set.

▼ A summer beach in the Crimean resort of Yalta. Seaside holiday spots are found all over the warm south, but there are also many beaches on rivers away from the sea, where people can relax without travelling far from home. At the end of the Second World War, a famous meeting took place in Yalta between President Roosevelt of the United States, Britain's Winston Churchill and the Soviet leader, Stalin.

▲ The Soviet Union is the most successful of all nations at the Olympic Games. The Olympics of 1980 were staged mainly in Moscow's Lenin Stadium, seen here.

▼ The Soviet Union has astonished the world on numerous occasions at international sports events with the brilliance and grace of young gymnasts like Olga Korbut and Nelli Kim.

Gazetteer

Alma Ata Capital of Kazakhstan at the junction of Central Asia and Siberia, not far from the Chinese border. A green valley oasis-city, its name means 'Father of Apples'. Built by Russians in 1854 as a city fortress and an outpost against China.

Ashkhabad Capital of Turkmenia at the most southerly point of the country, on the edge of the Kara Kum (Black Sands) desert and in the foothills of the Kopet Dag Mountains. Built by Russians in 1881 as an outpost against the Turks.

Azov Sea In the south of European Russia, it is connected with the Black Sea by the Kerch Straits. Some 15 m deep and 38 000 sq km in area, part of it is frozen from November to March.

Baikal, Lake Situated in the mountains of southern Siberia, it is one of nature's wonders, being the world's deepest lake: 1620 m, and Asia's largest freshwater lake.

Baku Capital of Azerbaidzhan, port on the Caspian Sea and oil centre in the Caucasus; at the turn of the century it was the world's largest producer of oil. Dates back to the 5th century, becoming part of Russia in 1806. Now famous for oil drilling and refining, and one of the most famous scientific centres in the USSR.

Caspian Sea Forms a boundary in the south between Europe and Asia, sharing a shore with Iran. It is the world's largest inland sea: 371 0000 sq km, maximum depth 1025 m.

Caucasus A great mountain range that extends between the Black and the Caspian seas. Its highest mountain is Mt Elbrus (5642m), some 835 m higher than Mt Blanc and Europe's tallest.

Dnepr River Flows down from the Valdai Hills west of Moscow through the Ukraine to the Black Sea for 2250 km, the third longest river in Europe after the Volga and Danube.

Don River Rises in the central Russian uplands and flows southeastwards towards the Volga, to which it is now linked by the Volga-Don Canal, and empties into the Azov Sea.

Dushanbe Capital of Tadzhikistan on the country's southern frontier with Afghanistan. Ringed by mountains, the city has developed only since 1924, before which it was a market held on Mondays—hence the city's name which means 'Monday'.

Frunze Capital of Kirgizia, it was founded in early 19th century as a Russian fort against China. The town, Pishpek (meaning 'five fingers' after the five mountain peaks around it), was renamed Frunze in 1926 after the Soviet army leader Mikhail Frunze.

Kiev Capital of the Ukraine and 'mother of all Russian cities' since it formed the centre of the first Russian state in the 9th century and was on the road 'from the Vikings to the Greeks'. It lies on the middle reaches of the Dnepr River and is now a most beautiful garden-city after being virtually razed in the last war.

Kishinyov Capital of Moldavia, it has had a colourful past: since it became known in 1420 it was Turkish in the 16th century, Russian in 1812 as the capital of Bessarabia, Rumanian from 1918 to 1944, and Soviet from the end of the last war. Famous for its food, wine and tobacco industries.

Lena River One of Siberia's longest rivers (4300 km), rising west of Lake Baikal. Despite the cold, it is navigable almost throughout its course for five months in the year, carrying Siberia's furs, timber and gold.

Leningrad Founded in 1703 by Peter the Great, it was Russia's capital city, first as Saint Petersburg, then Petrograd, until 1918. It is now the USSR's second city, with some 5 million inhabitants, yet is still the most beautiful metropolis in the country with its famous Winter Palace and Hermitage Museum, and many fine palaces and avenues. It stands at the head of the Gulf of Finland on both banks of the Neva River.

Minsk Capital of Belorussia, it dates back to 1067, and for long periods was the cultural centre of Lithuania. It became Russian in 1793 and Belorussia's capital in 1918. Destroyed by the Nazis in the last war, it has now become a fine modern city.

Moscow Capital of Russia and the USSR, it dates back to 1147. It lies on both banks of the Moscow River, and is closer than Leningrad to the Asiatic part of the country and so has a more colourful population. The Kremlin (meaning wooden fort) is the centre of the city, and forms the site for the Soviet Parliament. While Saint Petersburg was the aristocratic city, Moscow was the merchant city, with much of Russia's industrial expansion in the last century directed from there.

Okhotsk Sea Inlet of the North Pacific Ocean in the Soviet Far East, it is divided from the Ocean by the Kamchatka Peninsula and the Kurile Islands.

Onega, Lake Second largest lake in Europe, in north-west Russia. It is linked by the Svir River with the Baltic Sea and Lake Ladoga, and by the White Sea-Baltic Canal and the Volga-Baltic Waterway with the White Sea and the Volga River.

Riga Capital of Latvia, it is an important old Baltic port, dating back to 1201 and passing from Livonia to Poland, then Sweden and, finally, Russia in 1721. Capital of independent Latvia between 1918 and 1939, it became Soviet in 1939. Now famous for shipbuilding, and radio electronics.

Tallinn Capital of Estonia, it was formerly known as Reval. Like Riga, it passed through many hands before becoming Russian in 1710 as a naval base on the Gulf of Finland. It is one of the country's most cultured cities.

Tashkent Capital of Uzbekistan, it is the biggest city in Soviet Central Asia. It was founded in the 7th century as a trading centre on the caravan route to China. Originally an oasis in the middle course of the Syr Darya River, it has long been prone to earthquakes and suffered much destruction in 1964. It became Russian in 1864.

Tbilisi Capital of Georgia, it has been known since the 4th century and has been the Georgian capital since the 6th century. It became Russian in 1801 and for a time was called Tiflis—since it was said, the Russian tsar could not pronounce Tbilisi. The city is an ancient cultural centre and a treasury of Georgian architecture, including 5–7th century churches.

Ural Mountains Range of high hills dividing Europe and Asia, and the Russian plain from the West Siberian lowland. Its highest peak is Mt Narodnaya: 1894 m. The chain stretches from the Arctic Ocean down to the Central Asian deserts.

Vilnius Capital of Lithuania, it used to be called Vilna. It has been known since the 12th century and became Lithuania's capital in 1323. At first Russian Orthodox, it became Polish Catholic in the 17th century; during 17–19th centuries it was Europe's centre of Jewish culture. Vilnius became Russian in 1795 and Soviet in 1939.

Volga River The 'Mother' of all Russian rivers, the great Volga, Europe's longest waterway (3900 km), Like other Soviet rivers, it provides a vital water road for ship and barge cargoes and timber-rafting; it also turns the turbine rotors of hydro-electric stations, so supplying the country with electricity.

Yerevan Capital of Armenia, the city has as backdrop the twin Ararat Mountains across the border in Turkey and Iran. It has been known since the 7th century, and from 1440 belonged to Persia and Turkey; in 1827 it became part of the Russian Empire, but is today a thriving Armenian cultural and economic centre.

Index

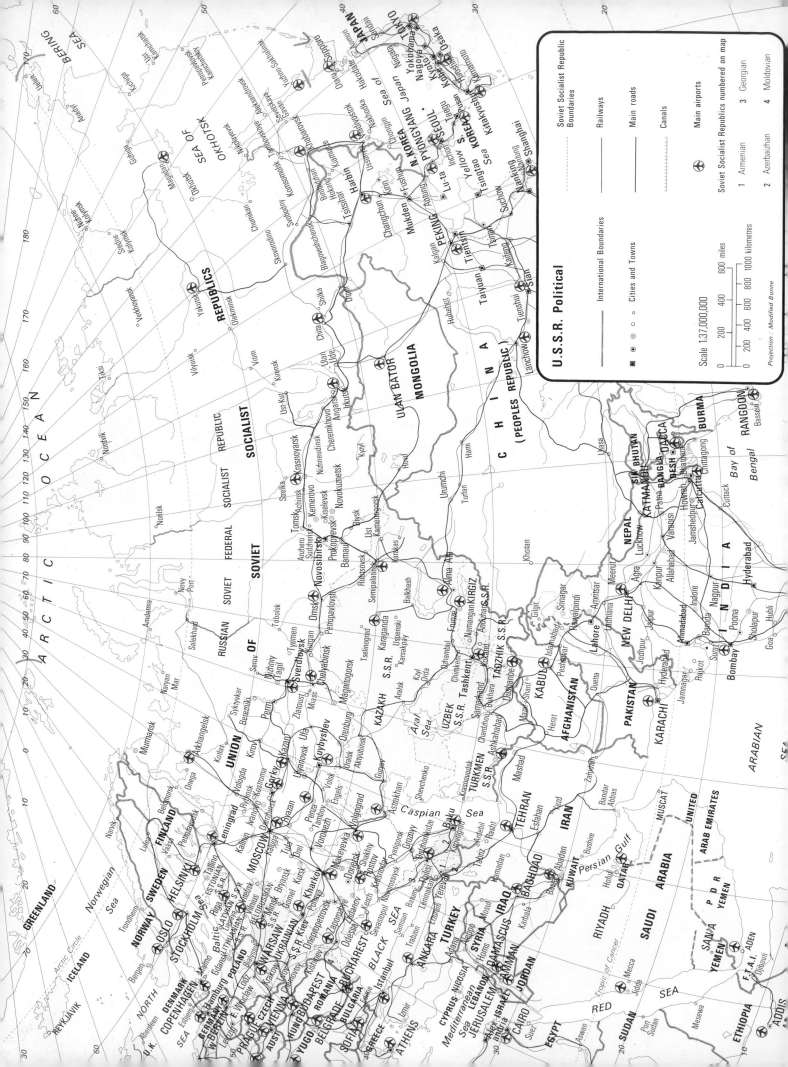

ARCTIC OCEAN

BERING SEA

SEA OF OKHOTSK

JAPAN
TOKYO
Yokohama
Nagoya
Osaka
Kyoto
Kobe

N. KOREA
PYONGYANG
S. KOREA
SEOUL
Pusan

SEA OF JAPAN

Sea of Japan

Yellow Sea

PEKING
Tientsin
Harbin
Mukden
Sian
Shanghai
Nanking

C H I N A
(PEOPLES REPUBLIC)

MONGOLIA
ULAN BATOR

REPUBLICS

SOVIET SOCIALIST FEDERAL SOCIALIST REPUBLIC

RUSSIAN SOVIET FEDERAL SOCIALIST REPUBLIC

UNION OF SOVIET

Krasnoyarsk
Novosibirsk
Tomsk
Omsk
Sverdlovsk
Chelyabinsk

KAZAKH S.S.R.

Tashkent
UZBEK S.S.R.
Samarkand
TURKMEN S.S.R.
Ashkhabad
TADZHIK S.S.R.
Dushanbe
KIRGIZ
Frunze

Alma Ata

Aral Sea

Balkhash

Lake Baikal

MOSCOW
Leningrad
Gorky
Kazan
Kuybyshev
Volgograd
Rostov

Kharkov
Kiev
UKRAINIAN S.S.R.

Caspian Sea

Baku

TEHRAN
IRAN
Esfahan

AFGHANISTAN
KABUL
Herat
Quetta

PAKISTAN
KARACHI
Lahore
Rawalpindi

NEW DELHI
I N D I A
Bombay
Hyderabad
Nagpur
Calcutta
Madras

NEPAL
KATMANDU
BHUTAN
SIK
BANGLA DESH
DACCA

BURMA
RANGOON

Bay of Bengal

ARABIAN SEA

GREENLAND

ICELAND
REYKJAVIK

NORWAY
OSLO
SWEDEN
STOCKHOLM
FINLAND
HELSINKI

DENMARK
COPENHAGEN

Norwegian Sea

NORTH SEA

Baltic Sea

U.K.

E. GERMANY
W. GERMANY
POLAND
WARSAW
CZECH
PRAGUE
AUSTRIA
VIENNA
HUNGARY
BUDAPEST
ROMANIA
BUCHAREST
YUGO.
BELGRADE
BULGARIA
SOFIA
GREECE
ATHENS

BLACK SEA

Istanbul
TURKEY
ANKARA

CYPRUS
LEBANON
SYRIA
DAMASCUS
ISRAEL
JERUSALEM
JORDAN
AMMAN
IRAQ
BAGHDAD

Mediterranean Sea

EGYPT
CAIRO

SAUDI ARABIA
RIYADH

KUWAIT
QATAR
UNITED ARAB EMIRATES
MUSCAT

Persian Gulf

RED SEA

SUDAN

YEMEN
SANA
P D R YEMEN
ADEN

ETHIOPIA
ADDIS
F.T.A.I.
DJIBOUTI

Tropic of Cancer

Mecca
Jidda

U.S.S.R. Physical

metres	2743	1829	914	366	183	0
feet	9000	6000	3000	1000	500	0

Below sea level

International Boundaries

⊙ ⊙ ⊙ o o   Cities and Towns

Mountain Peaks and Depressions (in metres)

▲ 9,232   ▶ -388

Scale 1:37,000,000

0   200   400   600 miles
0   200 400 600 800 1000 kilometres

Projection : Modified Bonne